Hermetic Philosophy

A. S. Raleigh

Kessinger Publishing's Rare Reprints

Thousands of Scarce and Hard-to-Find Books
on These and other Subjects!

- Americana
- Ancient Mysteries
- Animals
- Anthropology
- Architecture
- Arts
- Astrology
- Bibliographies
- Biographies & Memoirs
- Body, Mind & Spirit
- Business & Investing
- Children & Young Adult
- Collectibles
- Comparative Religions
- Crafts & Hobbies
- Earth Sciences
- Education
- Ephemera
- Fiction
- Folklore
- Geography
- Health & Diet
- History
- Hobbies & Leisure
- Humor
- Illustrated Books
- Language & Culture
- Law
- Life Sciences
- Literature
- Medicine & Pharmacy
- Metaphysical
- Music
- Mystery & Crime
- Mythology
- Natural History
- Outdoor & Nature
- Philosophy
- Poetry
- Political Science
- Science
- Psychiatry & Psychology
- Reference
- Religion & Spiritualism
- Rhetoric
- Sacred Books
- Science Fiction
- Science & Technology
- Self-Help
- Social Sciences
- Symbolism
- Theatre & Drama
- Theology
- Travel & Explorations
- War & Military
- Women
- Yoga
- *Plus Much More!*

We kindly invite you to view our catalog list at:
http://www.kessinger.net

HERMETIC PHILOSOPHY.

Thoth-Hermes is Kosmic Thought. Now we must differentiate between this Kosmic Thought and thought in the ordinary sense of the term. When man at this time uses the word thought, he has in mind that mental action which grows out of a sensation, that Intellectual Apprehension that follows a perception through the senses; or else, that Comprehension which grows up in the mind as a result of some previous Apprehension which survives in the memory, or the mental faculty, resulting in a spontaneous act of mentation. In either case the thought is the result of sensuous contact with an object in the sensible world. According to the Nominalists, all thought is of this nature, that is, mind generated through the act of contact with the Sensible World. However, the Realists hold another view. According to them there is a realm of Thought above the region of the Sensible World. This is the realm of Ideas of Plato, and of the Logoi of the Stoics. It is the realm of Kosmic Thought which is above all sensible Objects. It is, in a word, the Super-Sensible or Intelligible World. To understand this proposition, one must assume a Kosmic Mind, a sort of Impersonal Thinker, that is continually thinking Kosmic Thoughts, a process of Kosmic Ideation. This will give us the Logos of the Gnostics in its lowest aspect. It is this Kosmic Reason, that is not a person, but a Universal principle of Rational Activity. This Kosmic Reason, by reason of its very activity, is originating Kosmic Thoughts, and at any moment of time, the sum total of those thoughts will constitute the Intelligible World at that particular time. Thus we have a state of Kosmic Ideation precedent to the existence of the Sensible World. These Kosmic Thoughts are the causes of all those modes of activity which constitute the Things as they are, or Noumena; therefore these Kosmic Thoughts have a Real existence, whereas the sense engendered thoughts have only a nominal existence. To understand the problem, one must grasp the doctrine of the Indivisibility of Duration. This means the total repudiation of Mechanical Uniformitarianism. This latter view holds that the Universe is a Mechanism that moves as it is acted upon by a Force that directs it, and hence Duration is but a series of mechanical actions that eventuate in certain things that are to be apprehended through the senses and the Mind acting under the stimulus of those senses. From the former point of view the exact reverse is the case. The Universe is alive. Duration is the activity of a living principle that is ever acting upon Substance and in this way transforming it into an ever progressive sequence of new modes of life. This makes of the Universe a self-evolving Substance permeated by a self-evolving Life. From this concept we come naturally to that of Self-Consciousness as the first result of self-evolving Substance. Self-Consciousness being the essential characteristic of Living Substance, we must conceive of a Mind or Reason as the essence of this Living Universal Principle, an Abstract Thinking Substratum anterior to all things. This Kosmic Thinking Principle must, in the very nature of its being, generate Thought. Every such thought will be the Spiritual Word anterior to all that may spring forth from it. These Spiritual Words are the Logoi which are the realities back of the Sensible World. Thus we have the Living Process of Ideation engendering the Pure Ideas of the Ideal World. These are the Platonic Ideas. These Ideas acting upon the Plastic Substance or Materia, engender the Noumena, which are the things in their reality. The Sensible World is in reality the Subjective Picture that is presented to the Consciousness of the individual by the senses, and hence it is purely phenomenal, consisting not of realities, but of appearances.

Thoth-Hermes is the name given to the Living Process of Kosmic Ideation above outlined. He is at once the Scribe and the Instructor of the gods. This is only understood when we realize that there are two orders of gods. These we will call Kosmic and the Super-Kosmic gods. The Super-Kosmic gods are the Forces of the Pure Spiritual Realm, abiding back of the Manifest Universe. It is their activity that engenders this Sub-stratum of Kosmic Ideation. For this reason it is the expression as Living Consciousness of their activity. This Kosmic Ideation becomes the Scribe of the Super-Kosmic gods for the reason that all of its Thoughts are the Words engendering the Things of the Manifest Universe. This manifestation of the Super-Kosmic gods in the form of living forces that are ever evolving into Universal Form is the writing down of the Divine Words of the Super-Kosmic gods in the form of the Spiritual Words of the Principle of Kosmic Ideation. He is also the Instructor of the Kosmic gods, for the reason that they are but the Modes of Evolving Life growing out of the Kosmic Ideation. They are the Evolutionary processes that are engendered by Kosmic Thought, and therefore, the active manifestation of that very Principle. These forces of Creative Evolution, being the continual expressions of Kosmic Thought, are continually subject to its control, and are therefore said to be instructed by Thoth-Hermes. He is instructing them in the sense that the Writing or Spiritual Words of Hermes are to them spoken as the Intellectual Words, which therefore become the Self-Consciousness of those Creative Evolutionary Processes, or Kosmic gods, and therefore regulate their modes of activity. They are in this way made to act intelligently and not blindly. There is no such thing as a Blind Force in Nature. The Intellectual Words of the gods become the Living Words of the Forces of Nature, which have a determinate Destiny appointed to them in this way. The Living Words of the Forces of Nature cause them to act upon Matter in such a way as to impart to it the Vegetative Words which determine its growth, so as to order the development of the Universe in accordance with the Hermetic Writing. From this activity there is engendered in the Organized Universe the Sterile Words which have no power to introduce mutations in its form, but can only perpetuate that which has been established by the higher Forces of Creative Evolution. It is for this reason that there is no truth in the theory of Physical Evolution, Creative Evolution being the modes of the living manifestation of Kosmic Thought acting upon the Plastic Medium.

This being the nature of Thoth-Hermes, Hermetic, which is of the nature of Hermes, must in the very nature of things deal with the process of Kosmic Thought, that is, with Kosmic Thought as a Universal Principle, with the active process of Kosmic Thinking, and with the Kosmic Thoughts engendered by this thinking process. Hermetic Philosophy is the synthesis of those aspects of the Kosmic Mind into a Philosophical System. In a sense it is the Psychology of the Kosmic Mind. It must deal with Kosmic Thought both in its Essence as the Scribe of the Super-Kosmic gods, and in its Essence as the Instructor of the Kosmic gods. Hermetic Science is the relation of Kosmic Thought to all the processes of Creative Evolution worked out in detail so as to show the mode of evolving nature. Hermetic Art is the application of this knowledge of the mode of Creative Evolution to the practical work of controlling those very forces in a limited degree. Therefore its two principal departments are Magic and Alchemy.

The field of Hermetic Study is not the Sensible World but the Ideal World, therefore we do not follow the Inductive Method in any sense whatsoever. The Data accumulated through the activity of the senses is of no value. The beginning of our study is the Psychology of Thoth-Hermes. We must bring the Pure Reason and the Pure Intuition to bear upon the nature of the Sub-stratum of Kosmic Ideation, and must analyze the entire process of Kosmic Thought. After this, the relation of that Thought to the process of Creative Evolution must be traced out deductively. This will give to us the true understanding of the process of Evolving Life. This is what we might call the Hermetic Conception of the Universe.

The Hermetic Mysteries are the synthesized truth with reference to Kosmic Ideation, and the Creative Evolution which results therefrom, presented in such a manner as to veil the true meaning from all but the Initiate, and to reveal it to him. For this purpose, it is presented under the veil of Allegory and Symbol. Hermetic Initiation is two-fold. In the first place it consists in the unveiling of the Mysteries through interpretations so that the Mystae will be able to understand their meaning. This is done through the intellectualizing of the Mysteries. In the second place, it is through the gradual awakening of the latent faculties in the Mystae so that they are able to see the meaning of the Mysteries from within.

There are two classes of Initiates: The Mystae, who are learning the meaning of the Mysteries, and are in this way on the way to an understanding of the nature of Kosmic Thought, and the Epoptae who have reached the position where they are able to behold Kosmic Thought with the eyes of their understanding, and thus to read the writing of the Scribe of the gods. All previous training is to fit one for the task of reading the Writing, but the Epopt must read the writing, and in this way ascertain the nature of Creative Evolution and all the Mysteries of Nature at first hand. From this time forth he requires no Teacher, for the reason that he is able to read the writing, and therefore be taught by Hermes Himself. Such reading of the writing, which simply means the Intuitive Apprehension of Kosmic Thought in its pure Essence and of the diverse Kosmic Thoughts, is the meaning of being Initiated by Hermes. The Elder Brother is merely the Pedagogue who leads the Pupil to the School of Hermes.

When the Epopt has read the Writing of Hermes, that is, when he has acquired an understanding of the process of Kosmic Ideation, and likewise of the realm of Noumena engendering Thoughts, he must bring his Understanding to bear upon the Problem of Synthesizing the whole into an harmonious Unity.

When this work has been accomplished he will have mastered Hermetic Philosophy. Being now a Hermetic Philosopher, he must trace out the workings of the Forces of Creative Evolution, until he is able to grasp the entire process in a synthesized form, thus having a perfect comprehension of the entire realm of Hermetic Science. Having completed this work and thereby become the Master Hermetic Scientist he is ready to begin the study of Hermetic Art. To do this he must make use of the processes of Creative Evolution, which he now understands, in such a way as to accomplish practical results, in a word to carry on the work of Creative Evolution on his own account. To do this he must acquire the Hermetic Will, in a word embody the Living Word and make use of it in the control of the Forces of Nature and of Matter. When all departments of this operation have been mastered, and he has incarnated the Living Word and made it active unto the transformation of Matter he has mastered the Hermetic Art, and is, indeed, the true Hermetic Artist.

From the above it will be seen that Hermetic Philosophy is not a theory, or a School of Philosophy; it is a perfect Synthesis of Absolute Truth. It is the Mind of the Kosmos translated into terms of human understanding. The Consciousness of the Kosmos becoming a matter of Individual consciousness to the Hermetic Philosopher, he arrives at Kosmic Consciousness within himself. The teaching liberates man from the errors of Nominal and imparts to him Real Knowledge. It is, therefore, the Philosophy of Life of the Kosmos plus the incarnation of the Self-Consciousness of the Kosmos as a matter of Individual Evolution. The Epopt is therefore both a Mystic who has ensouled the Kosmic Self-Consciousness, and at the same time a Philosopher who understands the workings of Kosmic Thought as a problem that he has mastered. He is both the Thinking Subject and the Object of his thought.

CPSIA information can be obtained
at www.ICGtesting.com
Printed in the USA
LVRC030537050920
665109LV00005B/22